The Traditions of the Clergy Destructive of Religion
by William Bowman

Address:
HardPress
8345 NW 66TH ST #2561
MIAMI FL 33166-2626
USA
Email: info@hardpress.net

The Traditions of the CLERGY *destructive of* RELIGION: *With an Enquiry into the Grounds and Reasons of such Traditions.*

A

SERMON

PREACH'D at the

VISITATION

Held at *WAKEFIELD* in

YORKSHIRE,

JUNE 25. 1731.

BY

WILLIAM BOWMAN, M.A.

Vicar of DEWSBURY.

LONDON:

Printed for STEPHEN AUSTEN, at the *Angel* and *Bible* in *St Paul's* Church-yard.

MDCCXXXI.   Pr. 6d.

THE
PREFACE.

S the following Discourse
was not originally design-
ed to be published, I think
it neceſſary to inform the
World, that it now ap-
pears abroad in vindication
of it ſelf from the ill natured Cenſures and
groſs Miſrepreſentations of ſome of its
Reverend Auditors.

TRUTH has always appeared to me
in ſo amiable a Light, and Prejudice and
Bigotry in ſuch diſmal and deform'd
Colours, that I have long been uſed to
think it my Duty, upon all proper Occa-
ſions to endeavour the Advancement of
that, and Rooting out of this.

WHAT Succeſs I have had in the
preſent Undertaking, is evident from the
almoſt general Cry that has been raiſed
againſt me, and the ſevere Names I have
been branded with, for ſpeaking the Di-

ctates

ctates of my Conscience with freedom and
Sincerity.

'T I S indeed a hard Case, that Religion should be attended with such deplorable Circumstances, as not to be permitted the Test of Reason, but must be subject to the partial and obstinate Passions of perverse Men. Truth shines always the brighter for being opposed, and if what I have said may seem to cast some shade over it, a candid Expostulation from my Reverend Brethren would have been of much more Service, than the opprobrious Names of Erastian, Heretic, and Apostate. It is always a Presumption of a bad Cause, when foul Language is called in to supply the Place of Argument; and it was pertinently enough said by one upon this Occasion, that Demetrius and the Craftsmen might well be full of Wrath, when their Craft was in Danger to be set at naught.

T H E Subject of the following Sheets is the Result of an impartial Enquiry into the Nature of a Christian Church, which were designed as the Foundation of a much larger Work, which I purpose God willing, some time or other to publish:

publish: And I profess that neither Interest nor Scepticism, neither Ostentation nor Ill nature, but a hearty Love of Truth, was the Motive that induced me to speak out.

WHETHER what I have said be reasonable or no, the World must now judge, to me it appears so ; and if I have err'd, 'tis with a good Conscience, and a Readiness to retract upon sufficient Conviction. I have Reason to complain of the Misrepresentations my Sermon has suffer'd, and how many Things I have been made to say, which I never thought of. A Reverend Brother, who was many Miles off when it was deliver'd, has more than once preach'd his Audience to Sleep, in confuting Things I never advanc'd.

ALL I have to say to this is, that I have Printed my Discourse faithfully and entirely, as it was deliver'd from the Pulpit, without any the least Alteration ; chusing rather to trust the Candour of my Reader with any unguarded Slip that may be found in it, than undergo the Charge of a Falsification. I declare solemnly, notwithstanding what has been insinuated

sinuated by some of my Brethren, that I esteem and honour Episcopacy *as much as any one, as it is an Apostolical Institution, an Institution excellently adapted to the Circumstances of the Times, and an Institution settled by the Legislature ; but as to its being essential to the Church, I think I have Reason to deny. In a Word, as the Church of* England *by Law established is subject to the King's Supremacy,* (whose Power within his Realms of *England, Scotland,* and *Ireland,* and all other his Dominions and Countries, is the highest Power under God, to whom all Men, as well Inhabitants, as born within the same, do by God's Laws owe most Loyalty and Obedience, afore and above all other Powers and Potentates in the Earth *) *I have nothing to object against those Powers committed, by lawful Authority, to her Trust, and shall ever think myself in Conscience obliged to pay all due Reverence to her Dignitaries, and those of her that exercise any Jurisdiction.*

A S to what has been hinted, that I have borrow'd some Thoughts from the Independent Whig, *and* The Rights of

---

* Can. 1.

the

the Christian Church; *I answer, that 'tis impossible to write upon a Subject of this Nature, without saying many things that have been said before: As to the Books mentioned, I must own there are many Things incomparably well said, and much just and demonstrative Reasoning: And tho' I cannot agree with the general Tenour and Design of those Writers, yet where any Argument has appeared to me just and conclusive, and by Consequence is become my own, 'tis very possible, in treating upon the same Subject, I may have express'd the same Thought. I profess, I have no otherwise made Use of the foremention'd Books, than as the same Thoughts may have occurr'd to me naturally, and without a Design of copying. This, I think, will appear to any Judge of writing, from my different Method of handling the same Thoughts, and the Variety of Language in which I have expressed them.*

TO conclude, what Reception the following Discourse will meet with in the World, I neither know, nor care. I write for no Man's favour, nor fear any one's Displeasure: Truth, and the Cause of

pure

pure *Religion, with me, superfedes all o-ther Confiderations ; for the Sake of which I am content to face an Inquifition, or to ftarve in a Dungeon, to be* deftitute, afflicted, tormented, to wander about in Goat-skins, and Sheep skins, *to be flay'd with Scourges, or broken on Racks. Let Ignorance then, or Ill-Nature, rage as horribly as it will, let Cenfures and Perfecution purfue me even to Death, let my Reputation defcend down to fucceeding Generations branded with all the Infamy of Herefy and Mifcreancy ; yet while I live, there will be fomething within, will always fpeak Peace in the midft of a ftubborn and perverfe World ; and beyond the Grave, a* GOD *that will one Day reward thofe that have fuffer'd for Truth and Righteoufnefs Sake. Thus does it behove a Chriftian, thus a Minifter of the Gofpel, to act.*

E R R A T A.

PAGE 10. Line *penult. read* for a pofitive. Page 23. line 17. *for* later *read* former.

MATTH.

MATTH. XV. 6.

Thus have ye made the commandment of God of none effect by your tradition.

 IT has ever been the unhappy fate of Superstition, that by pretending to too much Religion, it has sapped the Foundation of all Religion; and by being productive of Traditions, that have no being but in a blind mistaken Zeal, it has levell'd the divine Oracles of the most high God, with the weak Opinions of frail Men.

PRIESTCRAFT has generally been reputed the Parent of Superstition, and as it is the undoubted Interest, so has it been the great Design of Priests of all Religions, to inculcate this profitable Delusion.

B   THE

THE Clergy of the Church of *Rome* had never rifen to that prodigious height of Grandeur and Glory, had not, by their means, Tranfubftantiation long ago juftled Reafon out of Doors; and the *Pope's Infallibility* been a more inconteftable Article of Faith than that *our Saviour died to fave finners;* to deny the Prieft's *power of Abfolution*, as damnable as *Adultery* or *Inceft*, and not *to bow to the Altar*, as *Murder* or *Rebellion*. All their pious Frauds and legendary Tales of Saints and Miracles, were confeffedly calculated for this end, to aggrandize the Order of an ambitious Priefthood, and to give them a dazzling Luftre in the Eyes of the Vulgar.

THE Paganifm of old *Rome* had never kept its Ground, nor its Priefts been had in fo much Honour and Efteem, but for their well projected Deceit of *Augurs* and *Haruſpices*, of the *Sibylls* and *Duumviri:* Their *Dies fafti* and *nefafti*, their *Epulæ* and their *Feriæ* were of infinite Ufe in the folemn Pageantry; and the removal of the profane Vulgar from their horrid Myfteries continued an awful Deference and Veneration.

THE

THE grand Impostor *Mahomet* had now slept undistinguish'd amongst the forgotten ruins of Mortality, and his Religion untalk'd of and unknown had perish'd with him, but for the pretended Visions he saw, and strange Voices he heard in the Cave of *Hira*, and his familiar Converse with the Angel *Gabriel.*

THE *Jewish* Doctors had never maintain'd the first Posts of Honour and Esteem, but for their diligently inculcating those abominable Traditions of their *Elders*, which *Grotius* and *Lightfoot* quote from their *Talmud* *.

WAS Religion indeed nothing but a politick institution, was there neither Revelation nor God in the World, this Procedure had been not only tolerable, but a well-concerted Scheme of future Greatness.

AND as long as the World was easy under this Priestly Domination, there was no mighty mischief done; or if a few of the wiser part of Mankind had found out the Cheat, it had probably been buried in their own Breasts. For who that has

---

* *Grot.* in Matt. xv. *Light.* Hor. H.

any,

any Regard to his own Welfare, to his Life or his Poſſeſſions, would endeavour to undeceive the World in a Point, in which it is every Man's Intereſt they ſhould be deceived?

BUT when we are ſure there is a God that *ruleth in the Kingdoms of the Earth* ; a God that hath revealed his Will by *many infallible Proofs* ; and hath tranſmitted a perpetual Memorial thereof to us and our Poſterity for ever; his Word is to be ſuppoſed ſufficient to direct our Lives and Converſations, and to guide us, without other Helps, *in the Way that leadeth to eternal Life.* All other Religious Doctrines and Traditions, beſides thoſe contained in the Divine Oracles, are the Doctrines of Devils, broach'd on purpoſe to affront the all-wiſe Majeſty of Heaven, by making him the Author of a Revelation imperfect, and incompetent for the End deſign'd.

IF the Loſs or Salvation of our Souls depend upon what God has reveal'd to us in Scripture, as I believe no Chriſtian will deny, then that Revelation muſt be ſufficient of itſelf for Salvation, or God is *an auſtere and cruel Maſter, reaping where*
                                                              he

he has not sown, and gathering where he has not strow'd.

NOTHING then can excuse an ambitious Priesthood, who tamper with the Consciences of Men, who preach up Doctrines unknown to the Scriptures, and *make void the Commandment of God by their Tradition,* who have more Regard to their own Greatness, than the Salvation of those to whom they preach, and who prefer their Authority over, to their Care of, the Churches.

WHAT shall be done to *these Watchmen that are blind, greedy Dogs that can never have enough, Shepherds that cannot understand, that all look to their own Way, every one for his Gain from his Quarter?* Can they say, with St *Paul,* they are *free from the Blood of all Men?* Or shall not rather the Blood of Numbers that have perished thro' their Default, be rigorously required at their Hands?

ONE would think it needless to enquire, whether the establish'd Church of this Nation laboured under the same Errors? A Church that calls herself pure and reform'd, and her Ministry orthodox and Apostolical. But alas! 'tis too true, that

that this our pure and reform'd Church wants yet Purity and Reformation, her Ministry is not so orthodox and Apostolical as is generally imagined; the Spirit of the old *Harlot* her Mother is not yet forgotten; the primitive Thirst for Grandeur and Ambition reigns sadly triumphant; the Honour of the *holy Function* is to be defended at any Rate, and the *Laity* to be deprefs'd to harmlefs Beafts of Burden, the innocent Creatures of Prieft-craft.

THERE are, without difpute, among the Clergy of this Nation, many moderate and brave Men, who make the *Gofpel of Chrift* the Rule of their Profeffion, and prefer *the Commandments of God to the Traditions of Men.* But then there are too many of a contrary Strain, haughty and enthufiaftic Men, who call themfelves, and thofe of their Order, the *Spiritual Princes of the Earth*, who wreft the Prerogative of God out of his facred Hands, who juftle Omnipotence out of the World, and fubftitute themfelves in its Place, *making void the Commandments of God by their Traditions.*

I SHALL

I SHALL therefore in the following Discourse endeavour to shew wherein the Clergy of this Nation oppose their vain and human Traditions, to the Divine Word of God. And this,

First, With Relation to their *Mission.* And

Secondly, With Relation to their *Authority*.

First then, With Relation to their *Mission.*

THAT there must be some to preach and expound the Word of God, as long as there is a Church and a Religion, seems to me necessary beyond dispute. For while Mankind is a Mixt Multitude of Ignorant and Careless, of Men of Business and Men of Pleasure ; while there are *Cares of the World, and Deceitfulness of Riches, to choak the good Word of God*, and render it barren and unfruitful ; 'tis necessary Mankind should always have a Monitor ready at hand *to preach the Word, to be instant in Season, and out of Season* ;

Season ; to reprove, rebuke, exhort with all long-suffering and Doctrine. For *how shall they hear without a Preacher?*

IT is as necessary there should be some Form of Government; some kind of Discipline in the Church ; for without it there could be no such thing as Unity, which is essential thereto. All the difficulty is, what Rule ought to be observed in the Management of this Affair ; which must never be left to every one's private and discretionary Conduct ; for then might all be Preachers and no Hearers, all Governours and none to be governed. Some kind of *Mission* is absolutely necessary, for the Sake of Order and to avoid Confusion, for *how shall they preach except they be sent ?*

I KNOW that as our Church has Tenets and Opinions of her own, with a peculiar Stiffness in this Respect, so to oppose and contradict them, at this Time o' Day, is in her candid Judgment, a kind of *Erastianism* little better than *Heresy.* But regardless of a Name, and for the sake of Truth, I shall however enquire into the Foundation of her Traditions, and

endeavour

endeavour to set this Question in as clear a Light, as the Thing will admit of.

I THINK it is evident beyond all Dispute, both from Scripture and the earliest Writings of the Church, that the Apostles, after our Saviour's Death, by Authority committed to them, constituted an Order of Men, to govern and take Care of the Church, and to ordain inferior Ministers in every Place.

IT is no less evident, that this Order has been continued down in a long uninterrupted Succession to the present Time, and in all Probability may be continued down till Time shall be no more.

FROM this *Apostolical Institution*, our Clergy, desirous to persuade the World that they have something in them of so divine a Nature, as in an especial Manner distinguishes them from the rest of Mankind, draw this pleasant Inference in favour of themselves; *viz.* that *Episcopal Ordination is essential to the Church of Christ, that without it the pure Word of God cannot be preached, nor the Sacraments duly administred,* and consequently that there are no true Churches upon Earth, but those of *England* and *Rome.*

C   WHETHER

WHETHER thefe Tenets be confiſtent with Chriſtian Charity or no, that Charity *which believeth all Things, hopeth all Things*, that Charity *which judgeth not left it be judged*, I ſhall not now enquire. I ſhall juſt obſerve by the way, that in a Church, reform'd and eſtabliſhed by Law as ours is, under the Epiſcopal Oeconomy, 'tis an Inſtitution abſolutely neceſſary for the Call of ſuch as are to to be ſet apart for the Adminiſtration of ſacred things, an Inſtitution laudable and excellent in itſelf, and admirably adapted for the Conſervation of Peace, Decency, and Order. But that 'tis eſſential to a Chriſtian Church is not ſo eaſily granted.

IF Epiſcopal Ordination be an eſſential Call to the Miniſtry of the Goſpel; it muſt be ſo upon one of the following Accounts. Either

   1. A s it was inſtituted by the Apoſtles for poſitive and perpetual Ordinance. Or,

2. A s

2. As it conveys to those, upon whom it is conferr'd, some necessary Requisite for the Work of the Gospel.

As to the first, That it was instituted by the Apostles for a positive and perpetual Ordinance,

I SHALL beg leave to observe,

THAT as whatever is instituted by the Apostles for a positive and perpetual Ordinance, must be a necessary and indispensable Term of Salvation; so 'tis inconsistent with the Goodness of God, to hide and obscure such Ordinances in Darkness and Ambiguities, which are of such vast Importance to the eternal State of all Mankind. As long as our *God is a good and gracious God, full of Mercy and Compassion*, he cannot but make every Thing that concerns the everlasting Happiness of our Souls, clear, obvious, and indisputable. But that this concerning Episcopal Ordination is not so, I leave its most bigotted Patrons to judge. The present State of the Church of *Scotland*, of the reformed Churches abroad, and of the modern Dissenters in *England* is an

C 2

incon-

inconteſtable Evidence of this.   'Tis indeed a reaſonable Inference, that becauſe the Apoſtles inſtituted this Ordinance, and the Primitive Churches rigorouſly obſerv'd it, and conſequently that at that Time it was the beſt and moſt advantageous Inſtitution for the Church, therefore Circumſtances remaining the ſame, that is, as long as it continues the beſt apparent Inſtitution, it ought to be inviolably and religiouſly maintain'd,   But to ſay that becauſe the Apoſtles inſtituted an Ordinance, which was the beſt for the Church at the Time of its Inſtitution, therefore that Ordinance is to be obſerved even when Circumſtances are ſuch that 'tis the worſt and moſt detrimental Ordinance the Church can have, is an Argument worthy only of the *Hickes's* and *Leſlies* of the Age.

AND as certainly as the Tempers of all Men and Times are not the ſame, ſo certainly could not the Apoſtles deſign, that an Inſtitution adapted to particular Tempers and Times, ſhould to all Tempers and at all Times ever remain the ſame.

BESIDES

BESIDES, from the supposed Perpetuity of this Institution, a Consequence will naturally result, which will overturn the Foundation of all Civil Governments; the Destruction of which, we are sure, the Apostles could never design. For as it implies an entire Independence of the State, and is a discretionary Act of the Bishop, independent too himself (for a divine Institution is not cognizable by the Civil Power) it follows that the Government can exact no legal Security for the Behaviour of the Clergy, but what they themselves are pleased to give; that it can impose no *Oaths, Subscriptions*, nor *Declarations* upon them, nor can controul them in the full Exercise of their Function, in what Manner they shall judge convenient: Consequently they are not restrained by any legal Ties, from secret Treason, or open Rebellion: No Civil Deprivation can stop their Mouths; their Office and Character extends over all Men, and to all Nations, and submits to no Authority upon Earth.

THIS is indeed to divide a Kingdom against itself, to erect *Imperium in imperio* with a Witness, to reduce Civil Societies

cieties into a State of Nature, to refuse *Tribute, to whom Tribute is due, Custom to whom Custom, Honour to whom Honour ;* this is to dispense with *every Souls being subject to the higher Powers*, to lay the Honour of Majesty in the Dust, to *despise Dominions and speak Evil of Dignities.*

I KNOW 'tis a Position of Dean *Hickes* *, That *no Doctrine is to be be rejected for the severity of its Consequences*. But to make this Position true, it is necessary that the Doctrine from which such Consequences result should first be proved; for when the pretended Doctrine is uncertain, and equally probable of each side, the Severity of its Consequences is the greatest Presumption against it; but when the Consequences are such, that they absolutely destroy other, even self-evident, Doctrines, that pretended Doctrine must of Course fall to the Ground.

THUS is it, I think, manifest beyond Contradiction that Episcopal Ordination was not instituted by the Apostles for a positive and perpetual Ordinance.

---

* *Answer to* The Rights of the Christian Church.

2. THE

2. THE other Reason, why Episcopal Ordination is suppofed an Effential Call to the Miniftry, is, that it conveys to thofe, upon whom it is conferr'd, fome neceffary Requifite for the Work of the Miniftry.

I KNOW no other Requifite for the Work of the Miniftry, than Piety and Learning. The firft difpofes us to be ferious, devout, and confcientious in the Difcharge of our Duty ; the fecond ftores our Minds with ufeful Kinowledge, furnifhes us with Materials to dictate, with Elocution to perfwade, and with Examples to propofe, but does Epifcopal Ordination confer either of thefe upon us! Does Piety or Learning follow the Impofition of Hands ? Does either Ignorance or Immorality flee at the Bifhop's Approach.

IN the Times of Infpiration indeed and when the Working of Miracles was a neceffary Qualification for a Minifter of Chrift, the Apoftles, as men commiffioned by the Holy Spirit, by an immediate Communication of the fame Spirit, ordained others to fucceed them in the Miniftry, which could not be fupply'd without

out thofe extraordinary Helps, and Affiftances, which were convey'd to them by
the Impofition of Hands.

BUT now that Miracles have fail'd, and
Infpiration is no more, what have we to
do with extraordinary Helps and Affiftances? Can we expect the all-wife God to
confer an extraordinary Grace for an ordinary, tho' important Work?

Do any of us feel any other Motions
of the Spirit than a ferious, and devout
Thoughtfulnefs, for the Work we have
undertaken, which is indeed (as all other
good Thoughts are) the ordinary opera-
tions of the Holy Spirit? Do any of us
mean any other Motion when we profefs
ourfelves moved by the Holy Ghoft at our
Ordination? Do we not ftill find ourfelves Men of like Paffions with our *Lay-
Brethren,* fubject to all the Frailties and
Infirmities of human Nature?

NOR do I apprehend, that that Pro-
mife of our Lord to his Apoftles, *Lo I
am with you always even unto the end of
the world* *, implies any extraordinary
Affiftances to be given to the Minifters

---

* Matth. xxviii. 20.

of

of the Gospel, or any particular Call to the Ministry; but only, that wherever *two or three are gathered together in our Saviour's Name, there is he in the midst of them.*

THUS does Episcopal Ordination convey nothing to those upon whom 'tis conferr'd as a Requisite for the Work of the Ministry.

So that from what has been said, we may, without any Absurdity, conclude, that tho' Episcopal Ordination be an excellent Institution, 'tis no divine Ordinance, nor essentially necessary to the Christian Church. I know it will be objected that I have the whole Authority of the Primitive Fathers against me, who always speak of Episcopacy as of a Divine Ordinance, of perpetual Obligation.

BUT I shall take very little Pains to confute an Objection, drawn from the Sayings of Persons, in Favour of an Oeconomy they lived under. 'Tis natural for all People to like their own Constitution best, and to speak of it in the most pompous Manner. Besides why might not they be biass'd by the same pleasing Temptations of Honour and Grandeur,

D

that

that we are? Why might not they err, out of too furious a Zeal, as some of us have done? But what, if most of those Sayings we quote with so much Triumph, should imply no such Thing as the perpetual Duration of Episcopacy; and no more than that Episcopacy was the settled Oeconomy of the Church at that Time?

I Do not know a more sanguine Expression than that of St *Ignatius*, *Let no one meddle with any Thing, tho' ever so convenient for the Church without the Bishop* *. Suppose this, if you please, to be a Prohibition, that no one take upon himself the Office of a Minister, tho' his Ministry be ever so necessary for the Church, without the Bishop's Ordination: What can it imply but that Episcopal Ordination was at that Time the settled means of *sending Labourers into Christ's Vineyard* ?

I KNOW nothing more is implied in that Saying of St *Cyprian* †, *Farewel Epis-*

---

* Μηδεὶς χωρὶς τῦ ἐπισκόπου τι πρασσέτω τ῀ ἀνηκόντων εἰς τ῀ ἐκκλησίαν. *Ig. Ep. ad Smyr. Cap.* viii.

† *Actum est de Episcopatûs Vigore, & de Ecclesiæ gubernandâ sublimi & divinâ Potestate.* *Ep. ad Corn.* 59.

copacy

copacy, and the *sublime and divine Power of governing the Church.* And I could shew the same of most of the other Expressions that have been quoted to this purpose, would Time permit, or were it necessary.

To have done then with this Head; what I have before said with relation to Episcopacy, is supported and confirm'd by the known Laws and Statutes of the Realm; and by our own Oaths and Subscriptions, who have over and over acknowledged the *King's Majesty in all Causes and over all Persons, Ecclesiastical and Civil, to be supreme Governour.* The Proceedings of the Legislature imply an absolute Power to appoint what Rules and Orders in the Church they shall judge most convenient. Such is Episcopal Ordination at this Day; necessary indeed, but only as 'tis the best apparent Institution and the Will of the Legislature.

I Come now
Secondly, To shew wherein the Clergy oppose their Traditions to the Word of God with Relation to their *Authority.*

D 2

thority, and that in two Refpects, as they claim,

I. A POWER of making Laws and Canons.

II. A POWER of authoritative Abfolution and Excommunication.   But

I. As they claim a Power of making Laws and Canons.

IN the Infancy of the Church, when Chriftanity was confin'd to Corners, and Believers were few and inconftant, while the Princes and Emperors of the World continued Pagans and Perfecutors, the Heads of the Church had undoubtedly a Power of making fuch Rules and Laws, as were neceffary for Decency and Order, and to confine all, who were admitted into their Society, to the ftrict Obfervance thereof.

LAWS are as neceffary for the Church as the State, when therefore the fupreme Powers would take no Care about the Church, but only to perfecute and annoy it, 'twas neceffary fome Laws fhould be

made

made by thoſe, who were ſet over it in the Lord: This gave Riſe to the *ancient Canons and Apoſtolical Conſtitutions*, which have long been ſo famous in the World. But when Kings and Emperors once became Chriſtians, the Church of courſe began to incorporate with the State, and the Power of making Laws reverted back again to the old Fountain.

To the Clergy indeed was generally left the Management of ſuch Laws, as concern'd the Church; but it was only by Permiſſion from the Civil Power, and in them the Confirmation, and Execution ſtill reſted.

IF indeed the Clergy of any Nation have a Power of making Laws and Canons independent of the Civil Powers, if they can aſſemble together in Convocation, when and where they think proper, to enquire into Offences and regulate the Church, they are ſo far from being Subjects, that they are really the *Preſidents* and *Princes* of the Earth; *Kings* of *temporal Kings*, to whom all Mankind are Subjects. If they can do this, what ſhould hinder them from unthroning Majeſty? What ſhould hinder them

from

from making Laws contrary to Laws, and overturning Nations at Pleasure? It is a mere Scholaftic Quibble to fay, that all their Laws and Canons relate only to Spirituals, and that they pretend to no temporal Jurifdiction: For a Sanction of Rewards and Punifhments, is effential to every Law; and every external Act, in order to the enforcing a Law, whether it be Exclufion from the Communion, a temporary Penance, or a formal Recantation, is as much a temporal Punifhment, as Imprifonment or Death.   If they fay, their Laws are only about the Spiritual and everlafting good of thofe committed to their Care; fo, I fay, are all Laws whatfoever.   And if the Civil Power can make as good Laws for this End, as 'tis poffible for the Clergy to do; to affert this Power, is to multiply Caufes for a fingle effect, a monftrous unpolitical Scheme, which in other Cafes the Clergy will not allow reafonable.   What the Laws of *England* have determined in this Cafe, I need not mention.   But

II. THE

II. THE Clergy claim further a Power of authoritative Absolution and Excommunication.

BY authoritative Absolution and Excommunication, the Clergy sometimes mean an absolute Power of admitting into, or excluding from, the Kingdom of Heaven, whom they think proper; at other Times a Power of admitting them into, or excluding them from, their Society upon Earth, in a judicial way.

IN this later Case, I have shewed before they have no Authority, but what they derive from the Civil Power; as it appears likewise from the Procedure of all our Ecclesiastical Courts.

As to the ~~later~~, I shall speak to it, in a few Words.

As God has frequently declared in Scripture upon what Conditions Mankind shall be saved or damn'd, it can never be in the Power of any created Being to disappoint his eternal Purposes. Whether the Conditions of Salvation required by God, be performed or no, is known only unto him, and to those as-
sisted

fifted by his divine Infpiration. For which reafon the Apoftles were endued with a power of remitting and retaining Sins, as declarative of God's juft Judgments, by Virtue of their infallible Knowledge. But would fhort-fighted Men claim this Power, which only appertains to Infallibility? Would he fet himfelf in the Apoftle's ftead, with all his Ignorance and Infirmities? Nay rather would not he fet himfelf above, not only the Apoftles, but even that God himfelf, *in whom he lives, moves and has his Being?* Would he wreft the Scepter out of the Almighty's Hand, extort his Prerogative from him, and damn or fave, whom he has not damn'd or fav'd?

COULD the haplefs Flocks, committed to the Charge of fuch, be once made to fwallow this horrid Delufion, there is nothing wanting to eftablifh the tyrannical Domination of *Rome ;* our Revenues would foon pour in Millions upon us, and our Authority rife triumphant above the Powers of the Earth.

WOULD the Clergy be but once fo moderate as to mean no more by this than a conditional Abfolution and Excommunication,

munication, we would not diſpute or re-
fuſe it.   But then of what Uſe would
ſuch a Power in the Church be? Shall
not every honeſt conſcientious Chriſtian,
who endeavours to walk *worthy of his*
Calling, with a lively Faith in God's
Mercy, and the Merits of his Saviour,
obtain a full Pardon and Forgiveneſs of
his Sins, without the Prieſt's Abſolution?
Or ſhall not the wicked, without the
Thunder of his Excommunication, receive
the due Reward of all his Sins!

I SHALL now beg leave to conclude
with a Word or two, by way of Ad-
vice.

NOTWITHSTANDING what has been
before ſaid, the Work of the Miniſtry is
doubtleſs a great and important Charge,
and in the Management of which is required the niceſt Care and Caution. We
are ſent to teach and take Care of the
wandring Flock of Chriſt, (*and Wo be*
unto us if we preach not the Goſpel:) but
not to aggrandize ourſelves at their Ex-
pence, or grow rich upon the Spoils of
Superſtition. We are appointed the *Stew-*
ards of God's Houſbold, to give his Servants their *Meat in due Seaſon and Mea-*
E   *ſure,*

sure, and if we perform not this Charge as becomes faithful Stewards, our Master has threaten'd *to cut us in Pieces, and to give us our Portion with the Unbelievers.*

LET us then set about the Business, we are appointed to, in good Earnest, not with *Eye-Service*, as Pleasers of ourselves, but as the *Servants of God.* Let us make the Holy Scriptures, the Rule of all our Actions and Labours in the Lord. Let us beware of those false Doctrines and Traditions that have given so much Offence to Religion. They may serve indeed to create a superstitious Awe in the weak unthinking Part of Mankind, but, with all sober and wise Men they only reflect Scorn and Contempt upon ourselves. They will certainly one Day rise up in terrible Judgment against us, for the Mischief we have done with them in the Church, and the Dishonour we have cast upon God. 'Tis this Affectation of Power and Grandeur, has raised us so many Enemies in the World, and gave Occasion to a late attempt upon us, at the Thoughts of which we may yet tremble. Would we change this

haughty

haughty Note in Time, we have yet Friends ſufficient left us to ſtem the Fury of deſigning Men, and to fruſtrate all their Endeavours.   Would we yet take heed to the Miniſtry to which we are called, *God, even our own God would give us his Bleſſing*, and happy *is that Servant, whom his Lord, when he cometh ſhall find ſo doing*.   Which, &c.

F I N I S,

N. B. *Mr* AUSTEN, *Bookſeller in* St Paul's Church-yard, *has a large Collection of* MSS. *Sermons, of three eminent Clergymen lately deceas'd, left with him to be ſold for the Benefit of their Widows.*

BOOKS Printed for STEPHEN AUSTEN, at the *Angel* and *Bible* in *St Paul's Church-Yard*.

THE *Universal Officer of Justice*. Containing the general Power and Authority by Law, of the several Officers and Ministers following, *viz.* 1. Of Justices of Peace. 2. Clerks of the Peace. 3. Of *Custos Rotulorum*. 4. Of Commissioners of Hackney-Coaches. 5. Commissioners of Hawkers and Pedlars. 6. Commissioners of the Wine-Licences, &c. 7. Of Mayors and Bailiffs of Towns. 8. Of Clerks of Markets and Toll-Takers. 9. Of Sheriffs of Counties. 10. Of Under-Sheriffs, and their Bailiffs, &c. 11. Of Coroners. 12. Of Constables, &c. 13. Of Church-Wardens and Sidesmen. 14. Of Vestry-men. 15. Of Overseers of the Poor. 16. And Surveyors of the Highways. The Whole being collected from all the Books of our *Common* and *Statute Laws* written upon the Subjects. And render'd generally useful to all sorts of People. 8º.

The Works of *VIRGIL* translated into *English* Blank Verse; with large Explanatory Notes and Critical Observations. (The Eclogues and Georgics never before printed.) By JOSEPH TRAPP, *D. D.* 3 Vols 12mo.

The Doctrine of the most Holy, and Ever-Blessed, TRINITY, briefly stated and prov'd; with the Objections against it answered: In a Summary View of the whole Controversy. As it was delivered in the Cathedral Church of St *Paul*, at the Lady *Moyer's* Lectures, in 1729, and 1730. By JOSEPH TRAPP, *D. D. Minister of the United Parishes of* Christ-Church *and St* Leonard *in* Foster-lane. 8º.

Fundamenta Grammatices : Or, a Foundation of the *Latin* Tongue. By NICHOLAS FARMBOROUGH, *Schoolmaster of* Watford. The seventh Edition; revis'd by Mr N. BAILEY. 12º.

A *Rational Grammar ;* with easy Rules in *English* to learn *Latin:* Compar'd with the best Authors in most Languages on this Subject. *For the Use of His Royal Highness Prince* WILLIAM. By *J. T. Phillips, Præceptor to* His Royal Highness. The second Edition. 12º.

A Compendious and Methodical Account of the Principles of Natural Philosophy, as explained and illustrated in the Course of Experiments. performed at the Academy in Little-Tower-Street. By Benjamin Worster, A. M. The Second Edition, with Additions. 8º.

CPSIA information can be obtained
at www.ICGtesting.com
Printed in the USA
BVHW041505220819
556561BV00024B/6467/P